In Loving memory of our son Sahib ʾ ı
to start the book and who also enjʿ
hope you will treasure this book.

contents

introduction

To all my readers

Ever since the age of 5 and my first taste of roti and daal (chapatti and lentils) I
fell in love with my mother's cooking, and that was Punjabi cooking. I know my
passion for cooking is borne out of my passion for eating!
And ever since I can remember, I have always wanted to cook and entertain
family and friends. I know that our traditions and culture have had a big part to
play in our lives. Cooking and eating together always tend to be the focal point.
As I grew up and went to school I remember jumping at the opportunity to opt
for 'cookery' at the age of 14. Here I was introduced to a world of cottage pie,
pasta, pizzas, apple pie, fish and soups. This was a different taste to my mother's
cooking but one I relished. After this experience I had the privilege of
introducing my parents and unsuspecting guests to the delights of English food
(but that's for another book!)
Later, university introduced me to the exciting tastes of Malaysian, Italian and
Chinese cuisines. I shared a flat with six other girls, from different parts of the
world. We were probably the most well fed student's in England.
Our Italian flat cleaner taught me how to make a basic pizza base which I could
freeze and just take out when I needed it and add my toppings and voila, a pizza
in 15 minutes. We were the only students who could rustle up delicious and
easy meals on a student's budget.
At home I was taught the basics of Indian cooking by my mother. She taught
me that food was a way of sharing love. She expressed her love for the family
through the simple Punjabi food she cooked every evening. Mealtimes were a
way of strengthening bonds between loved ones. My Punjabi identity is partly
borne from the food that I ate as a child. And now I want to pass on that gift to
my daughter, Priya and to you my reader.

preparation

As with all cooking the key is to be organised and plan ahead. There are a few basic utensils, ingredients and spices that you will need. You should be able to get from a local Indian store, if not from your supermarket. Many of the spices come in the whole form or ground powders.

A few different sized pots with lids
Deep wok for frying - khari
Rolling pin
Wooden spoons
Grinder
Tawa or frying pan

flours/rice:
wholemeal flour - Atta
basmati long grain rice- chawl
corn meal flour- mukhi Atta

Lentils/pulses:
moong daal
channa daal
toor daal
masoor daal
urid daal
red kidney beans
chick peas
kale channe

Oils:
clarified butter – ghee
Vegetable oil

whole spices:

Black cardamom - black lychee
green cardamom - green lychee
mustard seeds- rye
cumin seeds - jeera
dhania seeds - coriander
fenugreek seeds- methi seeds or fresh leaves
Cinnamon bark - daal chini
dried red chillies
curry leaves
Bay leaves
ajwaan seeds

Spices:
Garam masala
Turmeric - haldi
Chilli powder
Dhania powder
Paprika
Cumin powder
Amchoor
Chaat Masala

time saving tips

1 kg Garlic
1 kg Ginger
1 kg Chillies
A few bunches of coriander

These are time saving tips and that I have done for years.
It can be a bit of a task initially but once completed, you
can forget about peeling, chopping and grinding daily.
Purchase approx. a kilo of garlic, ginger and chillies from
an Indian store if you can as it is less expensive and
usually fresher as they have stock delivered most days.
Just wash the chillies and dry in a tea towel. Take off
stalks and place in a food processor and grind until finely
chopped. Place into ice cube tray and freeze overnight.
Then simply take out and put the cubes into a freezer bag
and keep in the freezer until needed. One cube of each is
usually enough for most dishes but if you prefer less add
accordingly to taste.

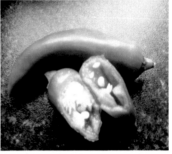

The same can be done for ginger. Simply break off all the
unsightly bits and peel all the individual pieces. Chop in a
processor and fill ice cube tray, freeze, tip into bag and
Keep till needed.

Garlic can be a bit tricky but one great tip that a friend past
onto me, is to break the garlic bulbs up and put into large

bowl full of water. Leave to soak for a couple of hours. Then when you take each clove out it
will be easier to peel. Do exactly the same as above and you will have enough supplies for at
least two months!

Wash the coriander and shake off excess water. Cut the stalks off just near the roots and chop
up the rest. Place into a freezer bag and freeze. Again, take a handful as required and add to
the dish. Alternatively you can buy ready frozen garlic, ginger and green chillies in any local
Indian greengrocers. Just use these as you would fresh ones.

One cube of frozen garlic is equivalent to three cloves of garlic.
One cube of frozen ginger is equivalent to one inch of ginger.

masala base (turka)

2 medium sized onions
½ tin of tomato, puréed
1 cube of garlic
1 cube of ginger
3 tablespoons oil
1 green chilli
1 ½ teaspoon salt
2 teaspoon garam masala
1 teaspoon turmeric
1 teaspoon paprika

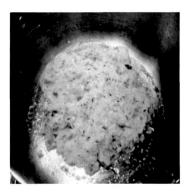

This masala paste is the basis of the sauce that forms the majority of Indian dishes.
You can make this quantity or I usually make it using 10 onions, 2 tins of tomatoes and adjust all the other ingredients. Freeze it little pots till I need them.

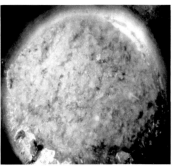

Heat oil and add onions, fry till golden brown and add the chillies, garlic and ginger. Fry till mixture is golden brown and then add the tomatoes and the spices. Cook for approx. 5 minutes till the oil comes to the surface. The Turka is ready to use.

This paste can be used for pulses, lentils and meat dishes. It can be frozen in batches. Simply defrost and reheat. Add the soaked beans, cover with water and cook in a pressure cooker for approx. 30 minutes. This will be covered in more detail in the other chapter.

For all meat and poultry dishes, reheat the masala in pot and add lamb or chicken. Cook for 20- 30 minutes adding little water from time to time to form a light sauce. Voila, a meal in under an hour.

light snacks

tandoori chicken

The classic dish of Punjab. What can be more appetising then sizzling tandoori chicken hot from the tandoor or oven with a crunchy salad and chutney.

Serves 6
2 lbs. Chicken, skinned and cut into pieces
2 green chillies
2 cubes garlic
2 cubes ginger
1 heaped tablespoon of cumin seeds
1 teaspoon coriander seeds
500gms plain low-fat yogurt
2 teaspoon salt,
3 teaspoon garam masala
2 teaspoon chilli powder
3 teaspoon lemon juice
3 teaspoon tandoori powder
Oil

Wash the chicken and prick all the pieces with a fork. Crush cumin and coriander seeds. Mix yogurt with all the spices, garlic, ginger and green chillies, and lemon juice. Add the chicken to the marinade and cover and leave in fridge overnight or for 2 hours at least.

Heat the oven to 200c and transfer all the chicken into a baking tray with a little oil. Cook in the oven for 25 - 30mins or until cooked through and golden brown.

Squeeze lemon juice over the top and sprinkle with paprika and garam masala. Serve with a green salad and naan.

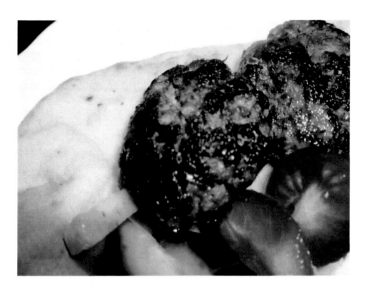

Lamb Kebabs

Aloo tikki & chole

lamb kebabs

Serves 8

2lbs minced lamb, 2 green chillies, 2 cubes garlic, 2 cubes ginger, 1 chopped onion, 2 teaspoons each of garam masala, salt, cumin powder, paprika and handful of chopped coriander.

Mix all the ingredients together and leave covered in the fridge for 1 hour to firm up. Divide up into 16 and make into a patty shape. Either grill for 4 minutes on each side or fry in a little oil in a frying pan.

Serve hot in nan bread and with salad or in a warm bun with relish.

chaat

This is a very popular starter and a light snack eaten during the hot summer months. There is no cooking involved, just assembling the ingredients. Also, there are no exact measurements. Needs to be made at the time of eating as the papri will go soft.

Serves 6

1 x 200gms box of readymade papri

1x 14oz tin of ready boiled chick peas, drained

2 potatoes boiled, peeled and cut into small pieces

1 pot of plain yogurt mixed with a little milk

1 teaspoon garam masala

 readymade tamarind sauce

Sprinkling of chaat masala, chilli powder, coriander, sevia

Pomegranate to decorate

Arrange the papri on a big serving platter. Mix the chick peas and potatoes with a little salt, garam masala and chilli powder. Scatter this mixture over the papri. Add salt and chaat masala to yogurt and spoon over all the papri and chick peas etc. Now pour over the tamarind sauce, sprinkle over the chaat masala, chilli powder, coriander and sevia.

Add as little or as much as you like of tamarind depending on taste.

Sprinkle on pomegranate.

amritsari fish

Serves 4
2 cod or haddock fillets cut into strips, 1 cube of ginger and garlic
4 tablespoons gram flour, 1 tablespoon of corn flour
1 teaspoon ajwaan seeds
1 teaspoon chilli powder, garam masala and salt
Lemon juice
Oil for frying

Marinade the fillets in lemon juice, salt, ginger and garlic paste and chilli powder for 20 minutes. Mix gram and corn flour with a pinch of salt, garam masala and ajwaan seeds. Add water to make a thin batter.
Heat the wok with oil. Coat fish strips in the batter and fry for 5 minutes turning occasionally till golden brown and cooked through.
Serve with a squeeze of lemon juice and chat masala sprinkled on top.

aloo tikki (potato patties)

Serves 4
4 boiled, peeled and mashed potatoes, 2oz frozen petit pois peas, boiled for 2 minutes, 1 teaspoon each of salt, chilli powder, cumin powder, amchoor powder and chopped coriander.

Mix all the ingredients together and make into 8 round patties. Dust in corn flour and shallow fry in hot oil in a frying pan.
Serve with chick peas curry and imli chutney or with mint yogurt sauce.

To make mint yogurt sauce: mix together 5 tablespoon plain yogurt, a little milk, 2 teaspoon mint sauce and chilli powder and salt to taste in a bowl. Aloo tikki is also served with chole.

pakoras (vegetable fritters)

Delicious served with mint or imli chutney.

Serves 6

8oz gram flour

1 medium onion

2 potatoes, peeled and chopped

2 teaspoon salt, garam masala, chilli powder

1 bunch of spinach washed and chopped

1 teaspoon coriander powder, cumin powder

Chop the onion and potatoes. Mix in a bowl with spinach. Add the gram flour and spices. Using a spoon add water to make a thick batter. Mix thoroughly. Heat oil in a deep wok. Take a teaspoon of the mixture and gently drop into the hot oil. Repeat until all the mixture is used up. Gently fry for 8-10 minutes till golden brown. Turn with a slotted spoon. Drain on kitchen paper.

Serve hot with imli or mint chutney

Mint chutney

In a blender, puree 1 green apple chopped, 2 green chillies,

1 bunch fresh mint, 1 teaspoon cumin powder, 1 tablespoon lemon juice, 1 teaspoon salt and tamarind sauce and some coriander. Add water to make a thick sauce.

Imli chutney:

Imli is tamarind. It can be bought readymade or can be made by boiling with water.

Take half a block of imli and boil in water for 5 minutes. Strain though a large sieve and discard the pulp. Add 1 teaspoon each of salt, sugar, chilli powder, amchoor, cumin powder and stir. In a blender

puree 1 tomato, coriander and spring onion. Add to sauce and chill for 30 minutes.

Both can be kept covered in fridge for up to a week.

chicken & lamb

butter chicken

This is again the classic dish of the Punjab. It can be made using left over tandoori chicken pieces or with fresh chicken. It has a rich buttery sauce which when served with jeera rice is so divine you will always want to make it for dinner parties.

Serves 4-6
3 tablespoon tomato puree
1 cube ginger
1 teaspoon cumin seeds
3 tablespoon single cream
1 teaspoon garam masala
1 teaspoon salt
3 dried red chillies
1 teaspoon dhania powder
1 teaspoon paprika
2oz unsalted butter
2lbs readymade tandoori chicken
coriander to garnish

In a jug add the tomato puree, salt, paprika and make up to 225 ml with water, stir.
In a pot heat butter and add cumin seeds and red chillies. When the seeds start to pop add the ginger, fry till golden.
Now pour in the all the ingredients from the jug in to the pot. Bring to a simmer and keep stirring in all the other ingredients except garam masala. Make sure not to boil as cream will curdle.
Add the chicken pieces. Cook till the sauce is slightly thickened. Finally add the garam masala and sprinkle over the coriander.

Serve with jeera rice or naan.

keema with cauliflower and chickpeas

Serves 6

1lb keema
1 onion sliced
1 teaspoon cumin seeds
1 cube of garlic, ginger
2 chillies
2 tablespoon oil
½ small cauliflower cut into small florets
1 tin of cooked chick peas, drained
½ 14oz tin tomatoes
1 teaspoon each of garam masala, turmeric, cumin, paprika, salt

Heat oil in a pot and add onion and cumin seeds, fry for 2 minutes, add garlic, ginger, chillies and fry for 2 minutes Add keema, salt, turmeric, paprika and cook on a medium heat for 15 minutes till keema is starting to go brown. Add cauliflower and cook for further 5 minutes with lid on. Add tomatoes, cook for 15 minutes and finally add drained chick peas. Heat through and add garam masala. Sprinkle with chopped coriander on top.
Serve with roti.

meatballs with boiled eggs

Serves 6
1 portion masala base, 3 hardboiled eggs
2lb mince lamb, 1 teaspoon each of: salt,
paprika, cumin powder, garam masala.

Mix salt, paprika and cumin powder with mince and form into golf sized balls. Heat prepared masasla base in a pot with lid. Once the base starts to simmer, carefully add the meatballs one by one in a single layer. Do not stir. Cover with lid and leave on a low heat for 6-8 minutes. Make sure the sauce does not stick, add a little water if it does. The meatballs will firm up and you can now stir. Cook for 20 minutes. Then add water to make gravy. Cut each egg into half lengthwise and add to meatballs. Warm eggs through, add coriander and garam masala and serve with jeera rice.

lamb with yogurt.

Serves 6
2 medium onions sliced
4 tablespoon oil
2 lbs. lamb on the bone in small chunks
1 teaspoon cumin seeds
1 black cardamom
½ 14oz tin of tomatoes, pureed
2 chillies
2 cubes of garlic
2 cubes ginger
1 teaspoon turmeric
1 teaspoon red chilli powder
2 tablespoon plain yogurt
1 tablespoon garam masala
Coriander

Heat oil a pot and add cumin seeds and cardamom. Add onions and fry till golden. Add ginger garlic and chillies and stir occasionally until all are mixed well and golden brown. Add in lamb chunks, salt, chilli powder and turmeric and stir well. Put the lid on and let the lamb cook in mixture for about 15 min stirring every few minutes.

The onions will start to break down and the lamb will become golden brown and release juices which will make part of the sauce. Stir in yogurt and cook for 5 minutes. Now add tomatoes, and leave for another 5 minutes until sauce develops. Now add 2 cups of water and cook with lid off for 10 minutes. The sauce will thicken and lamb should be tender. Add garam masala and fresh coriander. Serve with nan or rice.

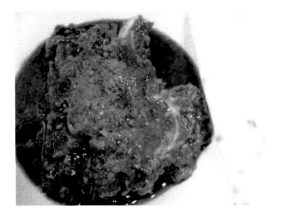

punjabi chicken curry

Serves 4-6
1 whole chicken skinned and cut
up into pieces (about 2 lbs.)
2 onions chopped
3 tablespoon oil
2 cubes garlic
2 cubes ginger
3 green chillies
1 teaspoon cumin seeds
1 stick cinnamon
1 black cardamom
½ a 14oz tin tomatoes, chopped
2 teaspoons salt
1 teaspoon turmeric
1 teaspoon paprika
1 teaspoon dhania powder
2 teaspoon garam masala
Coriander to garnish

Fry the cumin seeds, cinnamon and black cardamom in the oil to flavour it for a minute or so and the seeds start to pop.

Add onions and fry till nearly golden brown, add the garlic, ginger and chillies.

Fry for another 5 minutes till garlic and ginger are turning brown but not burnt. Add the washed chicken and salt, paprika, and turmeric.

Cook on a medium heat with the lid on for about 20 minutes till the chicken starts to colour.

After about 10 minutes add the tomatoes and cook for another 10 minutes. Add some water to make a sauce and mix well.

Cover and cook for 10-15 minutes, add the dhania and garam masala and coriander.

Serve with rotis and salad.

vegetables

bindhi (okra)

Serves 4

This recipe was passed onto me by my friend Sangeeta. She cooked when she came to stay with me and now I always cook them this way. There are many other ways but when you have tried theses bindhi I promise you will cook them this way again and again. It's so simple as well.

1lb bindhi's washed and topped and tailed and cut into 1 inch lengths, 1 small onion sliced, 2 tablespoon oil, 1 cube ginger, 4 dried red chillies, 1 teaspoon of turmeric, salt, paprika and garam masala. Scsame seeds to garnish.

Heat oil in a frying pan, add onions, sauté and then add chillies and ginger and gently fry. Add bindhis and spices, stir and cook on low heat for 10-15 minutes till cooked.
Do not put lid on as this will start to create steam. You just need to stir fry.

Serve with daal and roti.

stuffed kareles (stuffed bitter gourd)

Serves 5

Peel 5 kereles, keeping the shavings in a bowl, salt for rubbing, 1 onion, chopped, 1 chilli, 1 teaspoon of turmeric, chilli powder and garam masala, oil for frying

Make a slit along the length of the kerele but not right through it. Now take a teaspoon of salt and spread this along the inside of the slit. Repeat until all kereles are done. Leave for 1 hour. After an hour wash each kerele under a running tap to get rid of the salt and any bitter juices that may have accumulated. Dry with kitchen paper.
Meanwhile, make the filling, add a little oil to frying pan and add 1 onion, shavings of kerele's and green chillies and spices. Cook over gentle sauté for 5 minutes until cooked. Set aside.
In a wok add oil to deep fry the whole kereles. Cook for 5-7 minutes, turning the kereles so that they are golden brown on all sides. Take out and place into a serving dish. Now fill each fried kerele in the slit with the prepared filling.

Serve with daal and roti.

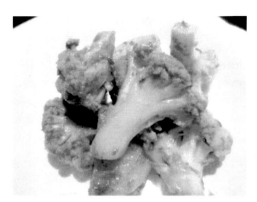

Aloo Gobi

Kerele

Aloo Began

Bindhi

aloo gobi (potatoes & cauliflower)

Serves 4-6
1 medium cauliflower cut into florets
2 medium potatoes peeled and cut up into 1 inch chunks
2 tablespoon oil
1 teaspoon cumin seeds
1 teaspoon salt
1 teaspoon chilli powder
½ teaspoon turmeric
1 teaspoon garam masala
coriander to garnish

Heat oil in a wok and add the cumin seeds. Once they start to pop, add the cauliflower, potatoes and all the spices. Stir thoroughly and put the lid on and leave on a low heat for 5 minutes. Stir every few minutes making sure the cauliflower does not stick to the bottom of wok. Cook for 10-12 minutes. The potatoes and cauliflower should be tender and cooked through.
Serve with daal and roti.

aloo baigan (aubergines)

Serves 4
1 large aubergine cut up into 1 inch chunks
2 medium potatoes, peeled and cut up into the same size as the aubergine
3 tablespoon oil
1 onion, chopped
2 green chillies
1 cube ginger
3 tablespoon chopped tin tomatoes
1 teaspoon salt
½ teaspoon each of turmeric, paprika
1 teaspoon garam masala

Heat oil in a wok and add onion and chillies. Fry for 2 minutes until onion goes golden brown. Add the chopped tomatoes and the spices and when the oil comes to the top add the aubergine and potatoes. Stir and cover the vegetables. Cook on a gentle heat for 5 minutes. Stir every few minutes to make sure that the vegetables do not stick to the bottom. Cook for about 10 minutes till aubergine and potatoes are cooked.

bhartha (mashed aubergines)

Serves 4

Bhartha is made from mashed aubergines. Traditionally in India where ovens are not used, the aubergine is roasted whole on the open fire until the skin is charred and black and could be peeled off with fingers. This imparts a smokey flavour. I now use a conventional microwave which works in the same way but you do not get that smokey taste.

1 large aubergine
1 onion chopped
3 tablespoon oil
2 chillies
1 cube ginger
½ 14oz tin chopped tomatoes
2oz petit pois peas
1 teaspoon salt,
½ teaspoon turmeric
1 teaspoon garam masala
1 teaspoon paprika
½ teaspoon chilli powder

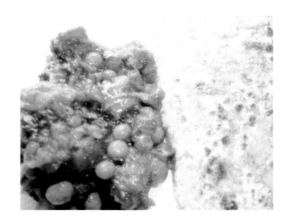

Put the aubergine in microwave on full power for 3 minutes, cook and then keep turning every 2 minutes till the aubergine collapses and is soft and partly cooked. This may take 6-8 minutes in total depending on size.

Top and tail aubergine and scoop out the flesh discarding the skin. Chop the aubergines fleshy part and set aside.

Heat oil and add chopped onion, chillies till soft and translucent, add ginger and cook till lightly browned. Add tomatoes and spices and cook till oil separates out and a sauce develops.

Add aubergine flesh and mash thoroughly as you stir and it's all mixed. Cook for about 10 minutes. Add peas and cook for further 2 minutes.

Serve with moong daal and roti or plain parathas.

aloo methi (fenugreek leaves)

Fresh methi leaves can be found at all Indian stores. Methi has quite a distinct taste so needs to be cooked through. Buy bunches and remove the leaves of the stalks. Wash and dry before using. Methi leaves can be frozen and added to chicken and lamb curries at the end to give a kick.

Serves 4
3 bunches of methi leaves, washed, dried and finely chopped
1 potato cut into small pieces
1 small onion chopped
1 chilli
2 tablespoon oil
little ginger
1 teaspoon salt
½ teaspoon turmeric
1 teaspoon garam masala

Heat the oil in a wok and add the onion. Fry till translucent. Add the chilli and ginger, fry for a minute. Add the methi leaves and potatoes, stir. Now add all the spices. Once mixed, cover and cook on a low heat for about 10 minutes or until potatoes are cooked.
Serve with masoor and toor daal and roti.

lentils & pulses

pressure cooker

The whole idea of using pressure cooker is to save time. It works by generating steam which then builds up pressure inside making the cooking process faster.

The pressure cooker is a very important part of Indian cooking but rarely used. You can buy ready cooked beans and pulses in tins at the supermarket. However, I still believe that the taste varies. When the masala base and lentils/ pulses are cooked together they penetrate the pulses giving a fuller depth of flavour.

There are just few do and don'ts with a pressure cooker.

Firstly make sure that you have enough water in the cooker as steam is generated and water is lost during cooking. Too little water and you curry will boil dry and burn.

Once the cooking time has finished, turn off the heat and leave for 15 minutes until all the pressure in the cooker has dissipated. If you open the pressure cooker too soon, there is a chance of an explosion!!

This method can be used for red kidney beans, chick peas and kale channe.

Wash and soak the pulses or beans for 6 hours before cooking.

Add one portion of the masala base into the pressure cooker and stir in your pulses or lentils. Leave to cook for 5 minutes on a low heat.

Add water, tighten the lid and put the weight onto the top.

On a medium heat cook for 5 minutes and then you will hear the whistle sound and you start timing from this point. Pressure cooking usually takes about 30 minutes. You will hear the steam every few minutes intermittently. Just leave the cooker until it is time to switch off.

When all the pressure has dissipated, (about 15 minutes) lift of the weight and any excess steam will disappear. Then you can open the lid. Finally add garam masala and coriander and serve with rotis.

moong & channa daal (whole mung beans & split chick peas)

Serves 6

6 oz. of moong daal

2 oz. of channa daal

2 teaspoon salt

½ teaspoon turmeric

2 tablespoons ghee/oil

1 onion

2 chillies

1 cube garlic

1 cube ginger

2 tablespoon tomato puree

1 teaspoon paprika

1 teaspoon dhania powder

2 teaspoon garam masala

Chopped coriander to garnish

Wash both the daals and place in the pressure cooker with 1½pts water, salt and turmeric. Pressure cook for 15 minutes on a medium heat. Once cooked, simmer on a gentle heat. In a frying pan, heat ghee and add the onions, chillies and cook till golden brown. Add the garlic and ginger and cook for 2 minutes and add the tomato puree and spices. Cook till ghee comes to the top. Now add this masala to the daal. Mix until the daal is a pouring consistency.

whole urid daal (whole black urid lentils)

Serves 4-6

This daal is regularly cooked at the Sikh temple every Sunday for the entire congregation to share and eat together. It is creamy, rustic, rich and a great accompaniment with roti and aloo gobi.

6oz urid daal, one portion of masala base, water

In the pressure cooker heat through 1 portion of the masala base and add the urid daal. Fry of 1 min and add about 1½ pts. water. Put on the lid and weight. Let the whistle sound start and then cook for 20 minutes. Turn off the heat and leave for 15 minutes.

Remove the lid and simmer the daal until it resembles a runny consistency and the daal and masala are all blended together. Stir in 1 teaspoon garam masala and fresh coriander.

channa daal (split chick peas)

Serves 4-6

This is the easiest daal to make and the tastiest as it has a creamy and nutty taste.

6oz channa daal, 1 teaspoon turmeric, 2 teaspoon salt, 4 dried red chillies, 1 teaspoon of cumin seeds, 2 tablespoons ghee and 1 chopped onion, 1 cube ginger, 1 teaspoon chilli powder and garam masala.

Fill a big pot with 2pts of water and heat. Add the washed and drained channa daal and all the other ingredients. Bring to a boil; simmer on a medium heat with the lid on for an hour. Stirring occasionally and add more water if needed. The daal should reduce to a thick consistency and the channa daal cooked all the way through. Check this by pressing a few peas in between your fingertips. If they are cooked they will flatten straight away. If not, add a bit more water and continue to cook. Finally add 1 teaspoon of garam masala and sprinkle in fresh coriander.

Moong & channe
Daal

Urid daal

Channa daal

kale channe (black whole chick peas)

Serves 6
8 oz. of kale channe
One of portion masala base

Soak kale channe overnight in water.
In the pressure cooker, heat the masala base. Add the washed and drained black channe and add 1 cup of water. Cover with a plain lid and cook for 5 minutes. Stir and add 2 pts. water and cook in the pressure cooker for 25 minutes.

After releasing the pressure, you should have a runny sauce and the channe should be cooked through. If there is too much water just boil off. Sprinkle with coriander before serving with rice.

rice & breads

rotis (chapatti)
Serves 3-4

Mix 2 cups of whole wheat flour and water together to make dough. The dough needs to be kneaded for 5 minutes to make it elastic. Add splashes of water if required but the dough should not be sticky.

Leave to rest for 30 minutes in the fridge, covered. Divide the dough into about 6-8 portions and roll each one into a golf ball in your hands. Heat the tawa or a non-stick frying pan.

Flatten one ball and dust your work surface and start to roll each disc out to about 5-6 inches in diameter. They should be round and of even thickness. Place onto the tawa for about 1 min till it starts to brown on one side. Then turn over and cook on the other side till bubbles start to form. The roti will start to puff up and you can do this on the gas hob with tongs or on the tawa. Keep turning over so you get a golden even colour all over but not burnt. Butter if you want. Wrap in a tea towel or foil to keep warm.

jeera rice
Serves 2-3

The key to making perfect rice is the measure of dry rice to water. For 1 cup of dry rice you will need 2 cups of water.

Wash 1 cup of rice and soak for 20 minutes. Then drain off the water. In a pot add 2 tablespoons of oil, 1 teaspoon of cumin seeds and 2 bay leaves. Let them sizzle and then add ½ a sliced onion. Cook till golden and then add rice. Stir to cover all the rice with oil. Add 2 cups of water and 1 teaspoon of salt.

Cook on a medium heat for 5 minutes and once the water starts to boil, turn the heat down and leave for 10 minutes with lid on. Do not keep stirring.

All the water should be absorbed. Turn the heat of and leave rice to stand with the lid on for 10mins. Sever with any curry.

cheats biryani

This a great quick dish when you have some lamb or chicken curry left over. Simply, fry 1 onion in 2 tablespoons of oil. Add 1 teaspoon of cumin seeds and a few crushed dried chillies. When the onions are lightly coloured, add the chicken or lamb pieces with some of the sauce. Mix and then add 1 cup of washed and drained rice. Stir till all the meat pieces are cover with rice. Add 1 teaspoon each of salt, paprika, garam masala and a few saffron stands. Finally add 1 cup of water and mix thoroughly. Cover and cook for 15 minutes on a low heat, stirring occasionally. When the rice is cooked, turn the heat off and leave for 5 minutes before serving. Serve with plain yogurt and a side salad.

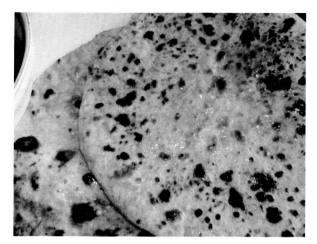

Roti

Jeera Rice

Cheats Biriyani

parathas

These are the classic breakfast or brunch eaten in most Punjabi households on a Sunday morning. Parathas are made of the same atta mix used to make rotis but have a filling thus making a substantial meal in one.
Use 2 cups of atta made up into dough, just like for rotis.

Serves 6

For **plain parathas**, just roll out atta as if you are making a roti, then spread a teaspoon of ghee or oil, on the roti. Then roll up from the top so that you have a cigar shape and roll this up like a Swiss roll and mould into a ball. Now roll out again to 5-6 inches. Cook on the tawa, on both sides and smear with ghee. It will become crisp and flaky.

Potato filling: 3 medium potatoes, ½ onion chopped, 1 chilli, 1 teaspoon garlic, 1 teaspoon ginger, salt to taste, 1 teaspoon garam masala, 1 teaspoon dried kasuri methi, 1 teaspoon crushed cumin seeds, 4 oz. cheddar cheese grated, ghee

Cauliflower and carrot filling: grate a cauliflower and 1 carrot and add salt. After 30 minutes squeeze out excess liquid and add 1 teaspoon crushed cumin seeds, 1 teaspoon garam masala, salt to taste and coriander, 1 chopped chilli and 1 teaspoon ginger.

Mix all the ingredients for the filling and taste to make sure it is seasoned well. Take enough atta and form a round ball. Roll out to a disc about 3 inches in diameter.
Put 1 heaped tablespoon of the filling in the centre of disc and gather up the ends and roll into ball, dust with dry atta and roll out to a round disc about 6 inches in diameter. Heat tawa and put paratha on and wait 1-2 minutes and lift with tongs and turn over. Once both sides are slightly brown use a spoon to brush on some ghee all over one side, turn over and do the same on the other side. Cook for a few more minutes till outside is crispy and brown.

Serve hot with plain yogurt and achar.

family favourites

saag (mustard & spinach leaves)

Saag is a delicious vegetable dish made from mustard leaves and spinach but you can add savoy cabbage and brussel sprouts. It is a traditional Punjabi dish that is a labour of love. When the harvest in Punjabi was plentiful, farmers would bring home the greens and the wives would make saag. Sometimes it is used as a test to see if a new bride can cook; if she can cook saag then she could cook anything.

The quantity of the ingredients for saag will sound like a lot but once it is cooked the greens do wilt. I often make a large amount and then freeze some of it for later.

1 savoy cabbage chopped
4 bunches of mustard leaves, washed and chopped
2 bunches of spring greens
1 packet of brussel sprouts
2 packets spinach
1 cup of water
1 tablespoon salt
4 green chillies
2 onions
3 tablespoon ghee
2 cubes garlic
2 cubes ginger
3 tablespoon fine corn flour
1 teaspoon garam masala

Wash all the greens under a cold running tap, shake off excess water and chop up.

In the pressure cooker add 1 cup of water and add the chopped greens. They will not all fit in at first but just keep adding a little at a time and with the heat, they will start to wilt.

Put on the pressure cooker lid and weight and wait till is starts to whistle. Leave on a medium heat for 10 minutes. Switch off the heat and leave for 15 minutes until all the steam has escaped. Take of the weight and slowly open the lid.

You should have a green mush and some water. Turn the heat back on low and start to boil away some of the excess water. Turn off the heat. Taking care, using a hand held blender, blend together the greens to a puree. Add the corn flour and stir.

In a frying pan, heat the ghee and add onions. Cook till golden and add ginger, garlic, and fry for a few minutes. Add garam masala and add salt to taste. Add this mixture to the puree and mix well together.

Serve hot with a knob of butter on the top with roti and yogurt.

Saag

Toor & masoor daal with rice and kerela

toor & masoor daal & rice (red split lentils)

This is the classic dish eaten in millions of homes in India every lunchtime. My children love it. It is simple. Light and wholesome and whenever we are fed up of fancy food, this just calms you digestive system. You can have it with suke aloo, achar and popadoms.

Serves 4-6
4oz masoor daal washed
2oz toor daal
2 teaspoon salt
½ teaspoon turmeric
1 tablespoon ghee/oil
1 cube garlic
1 teaspoon each of paprika, garam masala and cumin powder
1 teaspoon mustard seeds
4 dried red chillies
Coriander to garnish

Put washed toor and masoor daals in a pot and half fill with water, add turmeric and salt.
Cook for 20 minutes stirring occasionally to prevent the daal from sticking to the bottom.
The daal is cooked when pressed against the side of pot with wooden spoon, it is mashed.
In a frying pan add ghee/oil, mustard seeds, chillies, garlic and fry till garlic is lightly browned and seeds pop. Add spices, cook for 1 min and then add this mixture to cooked daal.
Stir and add coriander and cook for couple of minutes till all mixed together.
You just need simply boiled rice with the daal.

simple rice:

Wash and soak 2 cups of basmati rice.

Add 1 tablespoon oil to pot, then add drained rice and stir till all the rice is coated in the oil.
Add 4 cups of water bring to a boil and then turn the heat down. Cover and leave for 10- 12 minutes.
Stir just once and cover and leave for 5 minutes so that the rice fluffs up with the steam.

kharri and rice (yogurt & fenugreek curry)

This is the quintessential dish of Punjab. It has a distinct yellow colour and a sour taste. You can use leftover pakoras or make fresh ones.

1 pot of plain yogurt
3 tablespoons gram flour
1 medium onion chopped
1 cube garlic
1 cube ginger
1 green chilli
1 teaspoon of: dhania seeds, cumin seeds, fenugreek seeds, mustard seeds
2 tablespoons of oil
few curry leaves
2 teaspoons salt
1 teaspoon of chilli powder, garam masala, turmeric

Mix together the yogurt and gram flour in a bowl and whisk to a smooth thick consistency, with no lumps. Add salt, chilli powder, turmeric. Mix well and add 1 litre of water.
In a big deep pot, heat oil and add curry leaves. When they start to sizzle, add the cumin, mustard, dhania, fenugreek seeds and curry leaves and stir. Fry for 1 min and stir in chopped onion. Fry till golden brown and add garlic, ginger and green chillies.

Pour in the yogurt and gram flour mixture to the onion mixture and stir well. Bring to the boil and simmer for about 45 minutes until the kharri is reduced, thicker but pouring consistency.
Finally add the pakoras at the last 5 minutes of cooking. Sprinkle garam masala and coriander.

Serve with plain boiled rice.

matter paneer (indian cheese & peas)

Serves 6

For this recipe you can use fresh paneer or buy the readymade block.

To make fresh paneer, boil 4 pints of full fat milk in a pot and then add 3 tablespoon of vinegar. This will split the milk into curds and whey. Sieve the mixture through a muslin cloth in a colinder and you will be left with a soft cheese. Squeeze as much of the liquid out and leave with a heavy weight on top for an hour or so to make sure that all the paneer is dry. The paneer will be like a light crumbly cheese. This can now be used just like readymade paneer.

Cut fresh or readymade paneer in to ½ inch size cubes. Shallow fry in oil for a few minutes till the paneer starts to take on a light brown colour. Remove, drain and keep aside.

You will need:

1 portion masala base

2 potatoes, peeled and cut into small pieces

4oz frozen peas

Heat the masala base in a pot, add ½ cup of water to loosen the mixture. Add the potatoes and cover. Cook on a medium heat for 8 minutes until potatoes are nearly cooked. Add the paneer cubes and peas. Stir and cook for 5 minutes.

Add a little water to make a sauce. Sprinkle with coriander. Serve with roti.

chole and bhaturas (chick peas curry & fried breads)

A classic dish which is eaten when you want something filling and delicious.
You can either use 8oz dried chick peas which you will need to soak overnight or then boil in a
pressure cooker for 30 minutes before cooking. Drain off the water.
Or 2 tins of pre boiled chick peas, drained
Serves 4-6
2 tablespoon oil
2 onions, chopped
2 green chillies
1 cube garlic
1 cube ginger
1 whole black lychee
2 inch piece cinnamon sticks
1 teaspoon each of cumin seeds, turmeric, paprika, garam masala, chaat masala or amchoor
4 dried red chillies
½ a tin tomatoes, pureed
2 teaspoon salt
handful coriander

In a pot heat the oil and add the whole spices. When they start to sizzle, stir in onions. Cook until
golden brown and then add the garlic, ginger, green chillies. Cook till the mixture is browned and
cooked through. Add the tomato puree and the salt, paprika and turmeric. This is the masala base.
Once the oil start to come to the top and the masala is mixed well, stir in the precooked chick peas.
Cover with lid and leave to cook for 10 minutes. Add enough water to make a sauce. Finally add
garam masala, chaat masala or amchoor and coriander.

bhaturas (fried breads)

1 cup of self-rising flour   oil for frying
½ cup of Atta
2 tablespoon of yogurt

Mix both the flours in a bowl and add the yogurt. Mix and then add enough warm water to make
dough. Let dough rest in the fridge for 30 minutes and then make 8-10 golf sized balls, using a little
dry flour to make sure that the dough does not stick to the surface.
Now roll out with a rolling pin into a small even round, about the size of a saucer, (3-4 inches in
diameter). Fry each bhatura for a few minutes on each side until lightly coloured and puffed up.

rajma (red kidney beans)

This is again a very easy dish to make if you use the masala base. Rajma is best eaten with rice and suke aloo (dry fried potatoes). Rajma and rice is eaten in the north Indian state of Himanchal Pradesh when people go on a pilgrimage.

1 portion of masala base
8oz dried red kidney beans need to be soaked overnight and washed and drained.

Put the masala base into the pressure cooker and heat through for 5 minutes. Add the drained red kidney beans and mix well. Add 2 pts. water and then put on lid and cook under pressure for 30 minutes. After 30 minutes, you should have a pouring sauce and the kidney beans should be soft when squeezed between your fingers.
If the sauce is too runny, just boil for a few minutes to reduce. Garnish with coriander.

suke aloo (spicy fried potatoes)

4 potatoes cut into halves and then sliced thinly
2 tablespoon oil
1 teaspoon mustard seeds, cumin seeds, turmeric, chilli powder and garam masala
1 teaspoon salt
Slice the potatoes and wash and pat dry
In a frying pan, heat the oil and add the whole seeds and let them pop. Add the potatoes and the spices. Stir and cook over a gentle heat for 10-12 minutes until the potatoes are cooked through, crisp and golden brown. Serve with rajma and rice.

Aloo sabji & pooris

Chole bhaturas

potatoe sabji & pooris (potato & fried breads)

These potatoes can be served with any daal and rice. You can add dried red chillies as well, if you like them hot. This is another very popular dish in India and England as it can be a good brunch dish. Ideal with pooris.

Serves 4

2 tablespoons oil, 8-10 curry leaves, 1 teaspoon cumin seeds, mustard seeds, 1 cube garlic, ginger and 3 dried red chillies, 4 potatoes cut up into an inch pieces, ½ turmeric, 1 teaspoon of garam masala, paprika, dhania powder and a touch of amchoor

In a wok add oil heat and add curry leaves, fry for a few seconds and add garlic and ginger and stir until they take on a light brown colour. Add potatoes to wok and all the spices. Mix thoroughly and cook with a lid on for about 10 minutes until potatoes are cooked through. Stir occasionally and add a dash of water if needed to stop it sticking to bottom of wok.
Finally add coriander and serve.

pooris

These are little round rotis which are fried rather than cooked on a tawa.
Makes 8-10

2 cups of Atta, water and oil for deep frying

Mix enough cold water to Atta to make pliable dough. Set aside for 30 minutes.
Then heat oil in a wok and test it is hot by dropping in a small ball of dough and see if it raises to the top. Take about a golf ball size of the dough and make into a round circle, dusting with dry atta if need be. Roll out to the size of a saucer and should be thin and even.
Deep fry for a few minutes on each side till golden brown crisp and puffed up.

desserts & tea

sevia (vermicelli in milk)

Serves 2-3

Hot and sweet. Delicious after a spicy meal.

1 tablespoon of ghee in a pan, 4oz vermicelli, 1 pt. milk, 4 tablespoon sugar

Heat ghee in a pan and add crushed vermicelli. It will start to brown but keep stirring as it will burn easily. When all the vermicelli is a golden colour, add milk and sugar. Stir till sugar is dissolved. Bring the milk to a boil and then let it simmer on a gently heat until the vermicelli is soft and the milk slightly thick, about 10-12 minutes. You can sprinkle in chopped pistachio and almonds to give an extra crunch.

Serve hot.

This dish can also be served warmed up for breakfast in the winter.

gujrela (carrot dessert)

Indian carrot dessert serves at many weddings and festivals with ice cream.

The carrots are simmered to give a mellow and a melt in the mouth taste

Serves 6

2 lb. Carrots peeled and grated

1 pint of milk

6 tablespoons sugar

6 crushed up cardamom seeds

3 tablespoons ghee

2 tablespoons milk powder

2 tablespoons pistachio nuts chopped

The ghee gives the dish a glossy shine.

In a pot, heat milk and grated carrots, cardamom seeds and sugar. Stir to make sure the sugar is dissolved and does not stick to the bottom of the pot. Heat on a gentle simmer for 30 minutes till carrots are soft and all of the milk is absorbed. Keep stirring. Add 3 tablespoons of ghee and stir. Finally, add the milk powder and stir till mixed thoroughly. Cook for 2 minutes.

Transfer to a serving dish and sprinkle over chopped pistachio nuts.

Serve warm with ice cream.

Sevia

Gujrela

almond kulfi (almond ice cream)

Serves 8-10

6 pts. of full fat milk, 8 cardamom pods, 4oz sugar,
2oz ground almonds

In a deep pot heat milk till boiling and then turn down the
heat so that the milk is simmering. Keep stirring regularly to
stop the milk sticking to or burning at the bottom. Crush up 8
cardamom pods and discard the skins and add to the milk.
Add sugar and keep stirring till it is mixed in.
Keep the milk simmering till it has reduced by nearly half
and has started to thicken, about an hour.
Add ground almonds to the milk and continue to cook for another 10 minutes. Check sweetness now,
add more sugar if needed. Leave to cool. Pour into little ice cream moulds and freezer overnight.
When you want to serve, dip mould in hot water for 1 minute and turn out onto a dish.

kheer

Kheer always served as part of the langar (meal eaten at the temple) but it is delicious anytime,
anyplace.
3 pts. of milk, 1 cup basmati rice, 8 cardamom pods, 8 tablespoons sugar, pistachio, almonds to
decorate
In a pot add milk and basmati rice, washed and drained. Add crushed up cardamom pods without the
skins. Stir in sugar and continue stirring till all the sugar has dissolved. Let the milk simmer for about
30-40 minutes. Milk should have thickened and the rice cooked. Keep stirring to make sure it does not
stick at the bottom.
You can add chopped almonds, pistachio nuts
and sultanas at the end but I just prefer it plain
and simple.

mango surprise

Although, this dish is not from Punjab, it is a lovely way to have mangoes which are not always so sweet and as ripe as in India. Nothing can beat fresh juicy mangoes simply sliced.
Serves 6

1 large tin of mango pulp
1 banana chopped
1 tin of lychees drained and chopped
5 passion fruits, scooped out
handful of seedless grapes cut in half
1 pomegranate to garnish
1 small pot single cream

Firstly, whip up cream. Put all fruit into a serving bowl and add the mango pulp, stir. Finally add the cream and mix well. Serve chilled with pomegranates in top.

meeTe chawl (sweet rice)

Serves 4-6

1 cup of basmati rice, washed and drained

2 tablespoon ghee

5 cloves

5 green cardamoms

5 tablespoon sugar

few drops orange food colouring

1 oz. almonds, chopped

1 oz. sultanas

2 cups water

Wash the rice and soak for 30 minutes.

In a pot heat ghee and then add the whole spices and drained rice with a few drops of food colouring. Stir until all the rice is coloured and sauté for a few minutes. Add the sugar and stir until dissolved. Now add the water and stir. Cover with lid and leave to cook till all the water is absorbed, about 12 minutes. Now add the almonds and sultanas. Cover and leave on low heat for 5 minutes. Sprinkle over fresh coconut to decorate, if you want.

masala tea (chai)

Serves 4

1 pt. water

1 teaspoon fennel seeds (saunf)

2 black cardamoms, crushed

2 green cardamoms, crushed

3 tea bags or 2 teaspoon tea leaves

milk

Sugar to taste

In a pot boil water with fennel and black and green cardamoms.

Simmer for 5 minutes then add the tea bags or leaves. Simmer for another 3 minutes and then add milk. Bring to a boil again and then strain masala tea into cups. Add sugar to taste.

Nothing can end a delicious meal except a cup of chai.

Dear Reader,

I hope that I have given you some easy and simple recipes for you to start experimenting and adding your own touches.
I hope this book will encourage our younger generation to try Indian cooking and keep our wonderful culture and heritage alive.

Happy cooking & eating!

Nina